Read and EXPERIMENT

Experiments
with
MAGNETS

Isabel Thomas

heinemann
raintree

To contact Capstone Global Library, please call
800-747-4992, or visit our website www.capstonepub.com

Edited by Holly Beaumont and Mandy Robbins
Designed by Steve Mead
Picture research by Jo Miller
Production by Helen McCreath
Originated by Capstone Global Library Ltd
Printed and bound in the USA by Corporate Graphics

19 18 17 16 15
10 9 8 7 6 5 4 3 2 1

Library of Congress Cataloging-in-Publication Data
Thomas, Isabel, 1979- author.
  Experiments with magnets / Isabel Thomas.
    pages cm.—(Read and experiment)
  Summary: "Read and Experiment is an engaging series,
introducing children to scientific concepts. Explore the world
of magnets with clear text, real-world examples and fun, safe
step-by-step experiments. This book brings the science of
magnets to life, explaining the concepts and encouraging
children to be hands-on scientists."—Provided by publisher.
  Includes bibliographical references and index.
  ISBN 978-1-4109-7922-3 (hb)—ISBN 978-1-4109-7928-5 (pb)—
ISBN 978-1-4109-7939-1 (ebook) 1. Magnets—Experiments—
Juvenile literature. 2. Magnetism—Experiments—Juvenile
literature. 3. Science projects—Juvenile literature. I. Title.

QC757.5.T46 2016
538.078—dc23   2014041769

*This book has been officially leveled by using the F&P Text
Level Gradient™ Leveling System.*

Acknowledgements
We would like to thank the following for permission to repro-
duce photographs: Corbis: Erik Tham, 5; Getty Images: Doug
Armand, 11 (bottom), Joel Kiesel, 11 (top), Jonathan Kitchen,
7; Newscom: ZUMA Press/Nlu Yixin, 17 (bottom), ZUMA Press/
Richard Ellis, 15; Science Source: William D. Bachman, 21
(bottom); Shutterstock: Andresr, 27 (bottom), cristi180884, 6
(bottom)

All other photographs were created at Capstone Studio by
Karon Dubke.

We would like to thank Patrick O'Mahony for his invaluable
help in the preparation of this book.

Every effort has been made to contact copyright holders
of material reproduced in this book. Any omissions will be
rectified in subsequent printings if notice is given to the
publisher.

All the internet addresses (URLs) given in this book were valid
at the time of going to press. However, due to the dynamic
nature of the internet, some addresses may have changed, or
sites may have changed or ceased to exist since publication.
While the author and publisher regret any inconvenience this
may cause readers, no responsibility for any such changes can
be accepted by either the author or the publisher.

The publisher and author disclaim, to the maximum extent
possible, all liability for any accidents, injuries, or losses that
may occur as a result of the information or instructions in
this book.

ADULT HELP

Safety Instructions for Adult Helper
The experiments in this book should be planned and carried out with adult supervision. Certain steps should
only be carried out by an adult—these are indicated in the text. Always follow the instructions carefully.

Using Magnets Safely
All the experiments in this book can be done using ceramic magnets, horseshoe magnets, or ring magnets.
Wand magnets and horseshoe magnets are easiest to handle safely. Handle magnets carefully to avoid
pinching skin between magnetic objects, especially when experimenting with two or more magnets at once.
Stronger magnets, such as neodymium (rare-earth) magnets, can be dangerous and are not recommended
for these experiments. Keep all magnets away from bankcards, electrical equipment, and from young
children—they can be very dangerous if swallowed.

Using Batteries Safely
The electromagnet on page 22 should be built with a 1.5 V cylindrical "C" battery. Do not use batteries with
a higher voltage, and do not use a wire less than 3-feet long. Do not use rechargeable batteries, which can
draw a high current if short-circuited. Never insert fingers, wires, or any objects into a wall socket.

Contents

Some words are shown in bold, **like this**. You can find out what they mean by looking in the glossary.

Why Experiment?

Which **materials** are **attracted** to magnets? What is the best way to clean up oil spills? How do animals migrate thousands of miles without a map?

Scientists ask questions like these. They work out the answers using **scientific inquiry**—and the really fun part is the **experiments**!

Follow these steps to work like a scientist:

Ask a question.

Come up with an idea to test.

Plan an experiment.

What will you change?
What will you keep the same?
What will you measure?

Make a **prediction**.

Observe carefully.

Work out what the results mean.

Answer the question!

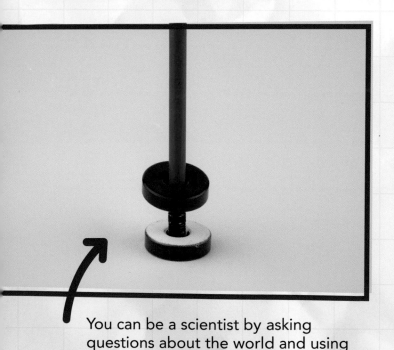

You can be a scientist by asking questions about the world and using experiments to help find the answers.

An experiment is a test that has been carefully planned to answer a question.

The experiments in this book will help you to find out more about magnets.

WARNING! Ask an adult to help you plan and carry out each experiment. Follow the instructions carefully. If you see these signs, you will need to take extra care or ask for an adult's help.

IS IT A FAIR TEST?

Most experiments involve changing something to see what happens. Make sure you only change one **variable** at a time. Then you will know the variable you are testing is what made the difference. This is called a fair test.

Get your eyes, ears, nose, and hands ready! You'll need to observe your experiments carefully and record what you see, hear, smell, and feel.

What Are Magnets?

Magnets come in many shapes and sizes, but they all have something in common. They **attract** certain **materials**.

These magnets can pull **magnetic** materials towards them. Magnets can also attract each other or push each other away.

REAL WORLD SCIENCE

People have found many ways to use magnets. They can be used for fun. They can also be used to solve problems, such as keeping a fridge door closed or stopping the pieces from falling off a travel game. Where else can you find magnets holding objects together?

Magnetic Force

Any push or pull is a type of **force**. The force that magnets create is called **magnetism**. Like all forces, magnetism is invisible. We can't see it—we can only see its effects.

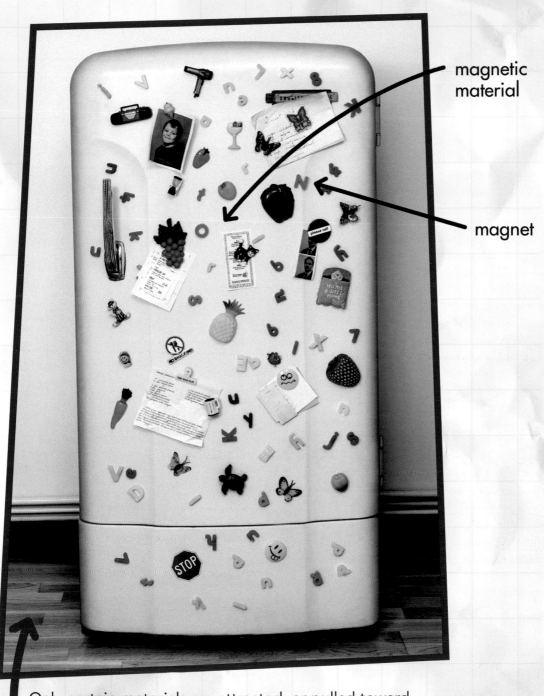

magnetic material

magnet

Only certain materials are attracted, or pulled toward, magnets. We say these materials are magnetic.

Magnetic Material Hunt

Which **materials** can magnets **attract**? Test a collection of materials and try to find a rule.

Equipment

- Different objects (nails, screws, nuts, forks, foil, jewelry, plastic, wood, coins, paper money, paper, crushed breakfast cereal, paperclips, door handles, pans, fabric, stones)
- Magnet

Method

1 Which materials will be pulled towards the magnet? Sort the materials into two groups. Write down the reasons for your choices. This is the idea you are going to test.

Magnets can damage electrical equipment such as computers. Never hold a magnet near anything that is powered by **electricity** or anything used to store information. **!**

2 Hold the magnet against each material in turn. Record your **observations**. Sort the materials into two new piles—those that are attracted to a magnet and those that aren't.

Material	Is it attracted to a magnet?	Prediction	Observation

Draw a table like this to record your **predictions** and observations.

3 **Analyze** your results. Were your predictions correct? Did any of the results surprise you? What links all the materials that were attracted to the magnet?

Conclusion

Did you find that only metals are attracted to magnets? If an object is **magnetic**, it must be made of metal or have metal inside. Some stones contain metal. Some paper money is printed with ink that contains metal, so it may be attracted to a magnet.

Did you notice that not all metals are attracted to magnets? Aluminium foil, silver jewelry, and copper coins are not magnetic. In fact, most metals are not magnetic. The most common magnetic metals are iron and **steel**.

Across Empty Space

If you want to push or pull an object, you usually have to touch it. **Magnetism** is a special **force**. A magnet can pull a **magnetic** object (or push another magnet) without touching it.

SEE THE SCIENCE ⬇

Use magnetic force for this "magic" trick. Make a simple paper insect, color it in, and hide a paperclip inside it. Tie the paperclip to a length of dark thread, and tape the end of the thread to the bottom of a glass jar. Hide a small magnet inside the jar lid. Put the lid on, then turn the jar upside down and carefully back over. What happens?

paper insect

thread

Magnetic "Magic"

In this demonstration, the paperclip is **attracted** to the magnet, even though they are not touching. Magnets can attract objects through air. Try the same trick, but fill the jar with water before you put the lid on. Can the magnet attract the paperclip through water?

Feel the Difference

Gravity is another force that can act even when objects are not touching. Gravity always pulls objects together, but magnets can create pulling *and* pushing forces.

Gravity pulls a skydiver towards Earth, even though she is not touching Earth.

REAL WORLD SCIENCE

In the future, magnets may be used to clean up oil spills in oceans. Tiny particles of iron can be added to oil to make it magnetic. Magnets would collect the oil quickly and easily, and the oil could even be reused.

Force Field

Objects do not have to be touching for **magnetic force** to pull them together or push them apart. But how close do they have to be? This **experiment** will help you find out.

Equipment

- Squared paper
- Different kinds of magnets
- Small iron or **steel** paperclips or nuts
- Ruler

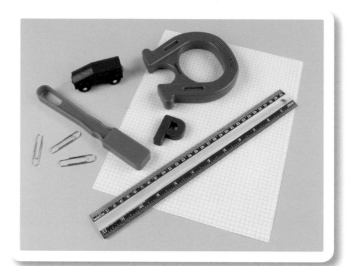

Method

1. Mark a line 6 inches (15 centimeters) from the edge of the squared paper, and line up the first magnet at zero.

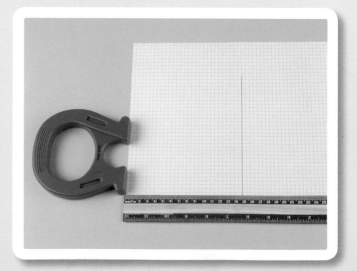

Place one paperclip on the line, at the 6-inch (15-cm) mark. Hold a second paperclip close to the first. What happens? Is the first paperclip acting like a magnet?

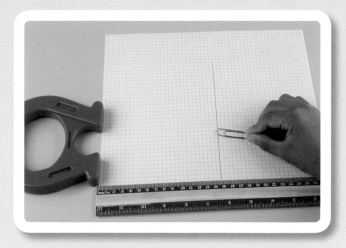

Move the first paperclip towards the magnet, ½ inch (1 cm) at a time. Each time, test to see if the paperclip can **attract** a second paperclip. When it does, record the distance on the grid.

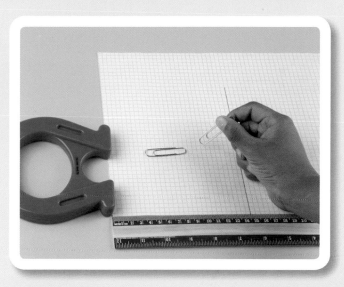

Keep moving the paperclip towards the magnet, ½ inch (1 cm) at a time. When does the paperclip begin to move towards the magnet without being pushed? Record your **observations**.

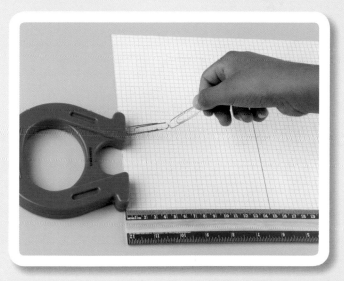

5 Draw a table like the one below to record your results. This will make it easier to compare them.

Type of magnet	Distance when paperclip began behaving like a magnet	Distance when paperclip was pulled towards the magnet
Horseshoe magnet		
Magnet on toy train		
Fridge magnet		
Wand magnet		

Predict: Will the distances be the same for the other magnets?

6 Repeat steps 3 and 4 using the other magnets.

7 **Analyze** your results.

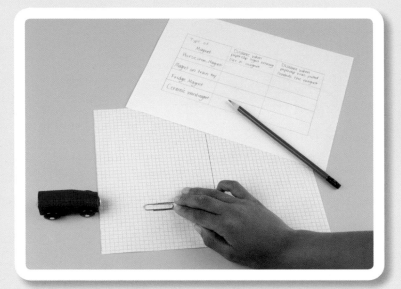

IS IT A FAIR TEST?

The **variable** you are changing is the type of magnet used. Everything else should stay the same. Use a fresh pair of paperclips (or nuts) for each magnet. The paperclips should be identical. Is it a fair test if a different part of each magnet is used to **attract** the paperclips? (Hint: **Experiment** 3 will help you decide). How could you improve your experiment?

Conclusion

The area around a magnet where its effects can be felt is called the **magnetic field**. Did you find that some magnets have a bigger and stronger magnetic field than others? When a paperclip is in a magnetic field, it acts like a magnet too and can attract other paperclips! The closer the magnet is, the bigger its effect.

REAL WORLD SCIENCE

Our planet acts like a giant magnet. Its magnetic field stretches far into space. The magnetic field is weak, but a magnet dangled on a string will line up with it. Some animals, such as monarch butterflies, can sense Earth's magnetic field. They use it to guide them on their long migrations.

A Push or a Pull?

The ends of a magnet are called the **poles**. Every magnet has a north pole and a south pole.

Magnets are made in many different shapes and sizes, but each one has a north pole and a south pole.

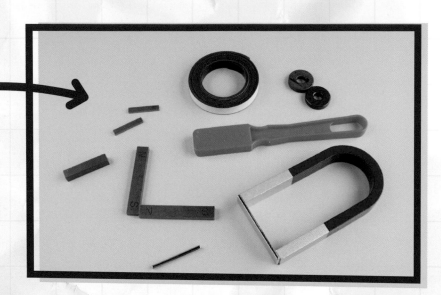

SEE THE SCIENCE ↓

Bring a magnet toward a **magnetic** object, such as a nail or **steel** can. What happens? Does it matter which end of the magnet you bring towards the object? Now bring a magnet towards another magnet. What happens? Does it change if you bring the magnets together at different ends?

Opposites Attract

The north pole of a magnet **attracts** the south pole of another magnet. The magnets are pulled toward each other and try to move together.

The north pole of a magnet **repels** the north pole of another magnet. The magnets push each other away and try to move apart.

Do not let magnets snap together. This can make them lose their **magnetism** and even break them apart. Strong magnets can also pinch your skin. Ouch!

SEE THE SCIENCE

Slide two ring magnets onto a pencil. Opposite poles attract each other. "Like" poles repel each other, and make a magnetic "spring". Can you think of any uses for a "spring" like this?

Two poles that are the same always repel each other. This is used in Maglev trains to allow the train to move along the track without touching it.

Test of Strength

Do some parts of a magnet attract magnetic objects with more **force** than others? Experiment to find out.

Equipment

- Magnet
- Small stickers (or a felt tip marker)
- Twenty small iron or **steel** objects, such as paperclips, nuts, or tacks

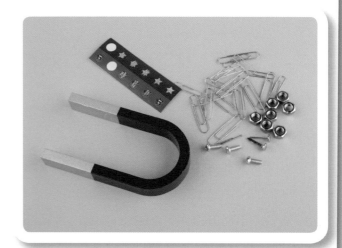

Method

1 Use the stickers or marker to mark four to six different spots on your magnet. You are going to compare the magnetic force at each place.

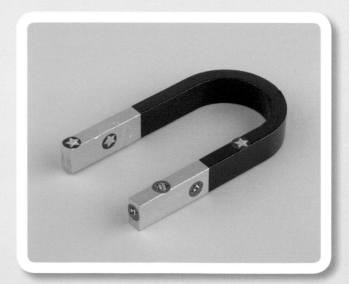

2 Hold the magnet off a table. Hold a paperclip against the first dot. Is it attracted to the magnet? Add a second paperclip. Is it attracted to the first paperclip? Add as many paperclips as you can to create a long chain. Record the final number.

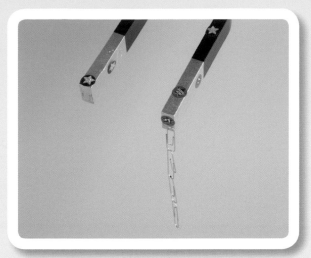

Predict: Will you be able to add the same number of paperclips to each of the other spots?

3 Remove all the paperclips from the magnet. Repeat step 2 for each of the other spots. Record your results.

 IS IT A FAIR TEST?

Would it be a fair test if you used a mixture of paperclips, nails, and other objects? Would it be a fair test if more than one object touched the magnet in each chain? How could you improve your experiment?

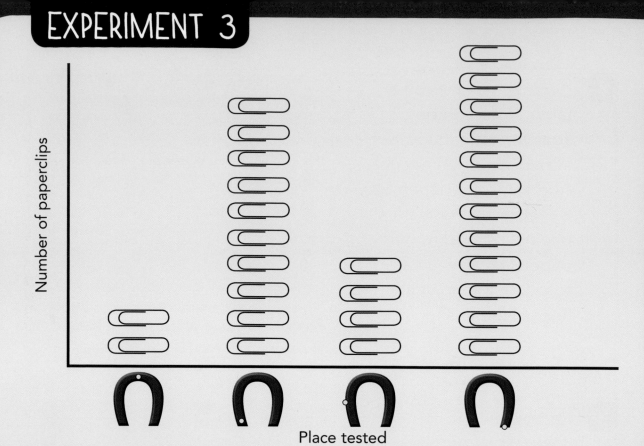

Number of paperclips

Place tested

Draw a pictogram like this to show your results.

4 **Analyze** your results. Which part of the magnet **attracted** the most paperclips? At which part of the magnet was the **magnetic force** strongest?

Try the same **experiment** with different magnets. Do you get different results?

Conclusion

Did you find that magnetic forces are strongest at the ends, or **poles**, of a magnet? A **magnetic field** is stronger in some places than others.

A magnetic field is invisible, but you can "see" it using this trick. Scatter some **iron filings** on a piece of thin cardboard or plastic, and hold a magnet underneath the card. The tiny pieces of iron will line up with the field. They show how the lines of force loop from one pole to the other.

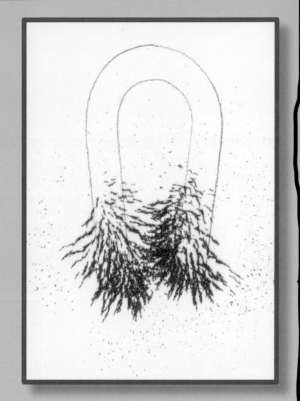

The closer each line is to the next, the stronger the force of the field.

REAL WORLD SCIENCE

Scientists use machines called magnetometers to measure the strength of magnetic fields. They can measure tiny changes in Earth's magnetic field, which can help to find resources like iron and oil, hidden deep underground.

Can You Make a Magnet?

Magnetism can be produced in different ways. The experiments in this book use **permanent** magnets. They are made of metal that has been melted, shaped, and cooled down in a strong **magnetic field**. Permanent magnets are always **magnetic**.

Temporary Magnets

You can make a needle magnetic by stroking it in the same direction with a magnet 50 times. Test your needle by holding it near another needle that has not been magnetized.

Needles are sharp, so handle them carefully. Don't drop a needle where someone could step on it.

Electromagnets

When **electricity** runs through a wire, there is a magnetic field around the wire. The magnetic field is stronger if the wire is coiled and even stronger if there is a piece of iron or **steel** inside the coil.

SEE THE SCIENCE ⬇

Connect the battery for a short time only, as the wire may get hot.

👍 **ADULT HELP**

You can make a simple **electromagnet** with a battery, 3 feet of **insulated** copper wire, and an iron nail. Wind the middle of the wire around the nail at least 15 times. Ask an adult to help you connect the ends of the wire to a 1.5 V "C" battery. Hold a paperclip near the nail when the **circuit** is broken and when the circuit is complete. What do you notice?

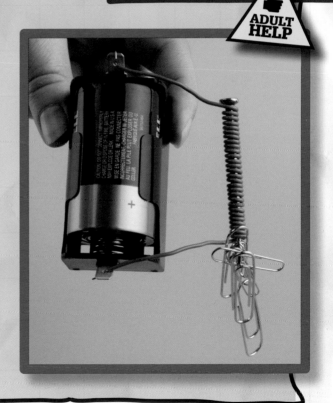

When electricity flows through the wire, the nail turns into a magnet. When the electricity stops flowing, the nail is not magnetic anymore. This makes electromagnets very useful as they can be turned on and off.

Can You Block a Magnet?

You've seen that magnets can work at a distance, through air and water. Can magnets work through other **materials** too? This **experiment** will help you to find out.

Equipment

- Magnet
- Long piece of thick cardboard
- Tape
- Paperclips, small nuts, or small nails that can be picked up by the magnet
- Collection of different materials, such as fabric, plastic, foam, wood, metal, cardboard

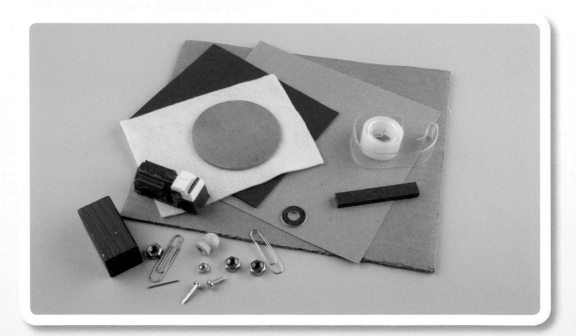

Method

1 Cut and fold the card as shown in the picture, to make a thin cardboard pocket with a narrow opening along the top.

2 Tape the magnet on one side of the pocket. Hold a paperclip on the other side. What happens? Does the magnet **attract** the paperclip?

If the magnet does not attract the paperclips when the pocket is empty, try using a stronger magnet or thinner cardboard.

Predict: Will the magnet still be able to attract the paperclips when each of the other materials is put into the pocket?

Material inside pocket	Does the magnet attract the paperclips through the material?	
	Prediction	Observation
Air	Yes	Yes
Paper		
Foam		

Draw a table like this to record your predictions and **observations**.

3 Slide each of the **materials** into the slot, one at a time, and move them around. Record your **observations**.

IS IT A FAIR TEST?

The **variable** you are changing is the material between the magnet and the paperclip. Everything else should stay the same. Is it a fair test if each material is a different thickness? How could you improve your **experiment**?

4 Insert your hand into the pocket. Record your observations.

Predict: Will the magnet be able to **attract** the paperclips through your hand?

5 Analyze your results. Which materials allowed the magnet to attract the paperclips? Which materials made the paperclips fall off? What do you notice about the materials in each group?

Conclusion

Many materials allow **magnetic force** to pass through them. Magnetic materials such as iron and **steel** do not. They interrupt the magnetic force by changing the shape of the **magnetic field**. These materials can be used as magnetic "shields."

REAL WORLD SCIENCE

MRI machines use very powerful magnets to let doctors "see" inside a patient's body. Steel chairs, bins, and even a forklift truck have been accidentally pulled into MRI machines. MRI rooms often have steel walls and doors to trap the magnetic field inside the room.

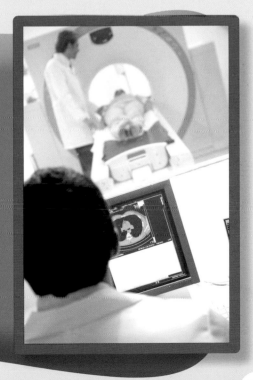

Plan Your Next Experiment

Experiments have helped you discover some amazing things about magnets. Just like you, scientists carry out experiments to answer questions and test ideas. Each experiment is planned carefully to make it a fair test.

Scientists are finding out new facts all the time. Experiments also lead to new questions!

Did you think of more questions about magnets? Can you plan new experiments to help answer them?

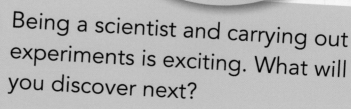

Being a scientist and carrying out experiments is exciting. What will you discover next?

YOU FOUND OUT THAT...

WHAT NEXT?

Magnets can attract **magnetic materials**. Magnetic materials are always metals, but not all metals are magnetic.

Are bigger magnets stronger? Plan an experiment to find out.

Magnets can work at a distance. They can work through different materials. The area around a magnet where its **force** can be felt is called the **magnetic field**.

Make your own **ferrofluid** by mixing **iron filings** with a small amount of vegetable oil in a glass jar. Plan an experiment to find out if it's easier to separate the ferrofluid or plain vegetable oil from water.

Magnets have a north **pole** and a south pole. Two poles that are different will attract each other. Two poles that are the same will **repel** each other.

Does joining two magnets together create a stronger magnet? Plan an experiment to find out.

You can make an **electromagnet** by passing **electricity** through a wire. If the wire is coiled, the electromagnet is stronger. If there is magnetic material inside the coil, the electromagnet is stronger. It is only magnetic when electricity is flowing through the wire.

Does the number of coils affect the strength of an electromagnet? Design an experiment to find out.

Glossary

analyze examine the results of an experiment carefully in order to explain what happened

attract pull on an object without touching it

circuit path through which electricity flows

electricity type of energy that flows from place to place through certain materials

electromagnet metal core made into a magnet by passing electricity through a coil of wire wrapped around it

experiment procedure carried out to test an idea or answer a question

ferrofluid fluid containing a magnetic suspension

force push or pull, which can make something start moving, stop moving or change its shape

insulated when something metal is covered in a material that does not conduct electricity

iron filings tiny pieces of iron

magnetic can be attracted by a magnet and can start to behave like a magnet itself

magnetic field area around a magnet (or a wire carrying electricity) where the force of magnetism can be felt

magnetism force created by magnets when they are near other magnets or magnetic materials

material what something is made of

observation noting or measuring what you see, hear, smell, or feel

permanent stays the same

pole one of two places on the surface of a magnet where the magnetic forces are the strongest

prediction best guess or estimate of what will happen, based on what you already know

repel force away

scientific inquiry method used by scientists to answer questions about the world

steel hard material made from iron and other materials

variable something that can be changed during an experiment

Find Out More

Books

Kuskowski, Alex. *Science Experiments with Magnets*. More Super Simple Science. Minneapolis, Minn.: ABDO Publishing Company, 2014.

Spilsbury, Richard and Louise Spilsbury. *Magnetism*. Essential Physical Science. Chicago: Heinemann Library, 2014.

Swanson, Jennifer. *The Attractive Truth About Magnetism*. LOL Physical Science. North Mankato, Minn.: Capstone Press, 2013.

Walker, Sally M. *Investigating Magnetism*. How Does Energy Work? Minneapolis, Minn.: Lerner Publications Co., 2012.

Websites

FactHound offers a safe, fun way to find Internet sites related to this book. All of the sites on FactHound have been researched by our staff.

Here's all you do:

Visit *www.facthound.com*

Type in this code: 9781410979223

Index